MY JOURNEY OF FAITH IN AN UNFORGIVING AND HOSTILE WORLD

Mary Joy

Mary Joy

MY JOURNEY OF FAITH IN AN
UNFORGIVING AND HOSTILE WORLD
Copyright © Mary Joy 2008

ISBN 978-184426-490-2

First published 2008 by
UPFRONT PUBLISHING LTD
Peterborough, England.

Printed by Printondemand-Worldwide Ltd.

Mary Joy

Introduction

This book is about my journey of faith, and how God has guided and provided for me during the last 40 years.

Life is not easy and I believe we need all the help we can get. With my faith in God, I have found the help I need for my journey. God has shown me the way I have needed to go. It has not always been easy and I have often held back but He has been very gentle yet firm with me, and to encourage me along the way

He has brought other people across my path to help me along the road.

(All scripture references are from The Bible, New International Version - UK, obtained from the website www.Biblegateway.com)

Mary Joy

Acknowledgements

Thank you Geoff and Christine Adams for your loving friendship and patience over the last 30 years. Thank you also for your help and advice when writing this booklet.

My thanks also to Jennifer Rees Larcombe for her help, advice and encouragement.

I would also like to thank the Rev. Philip Bell for his help and for recommending to me the Rev. Deacon Gill Kimber.

Thank you to the Rev. Deacon Gill Kimber for her invaluable advice and helpful suggestions on how to move forward into the publishing arena.

Mary Joy

Chapter One

We live in a cruel world. We are bombarded in the news about acts of violence towards people innocently going about their business. We see people with deep anger, people in pain with deep hurts, man's cruelty to man. We see a very harsh environment – the cruelty seems never ending and appears to be getting worse.

We only have to look at the state of our Nation to see that we have lost our way. There appears to be a breakdown in society. We see chaos all around us. The Government is desperately trying to put things right by passing legislation after legislation to stop the downward escalation. There is no time riper than now for Christians to stand up for their beliefs. We live in a multicultural society; our identity as a Christian Nation is being eroded by other faiths. Why isn't the Christian faith being vocalised and defended like other religions are? Why are we not making a difference? Why are we appearing to be the underdogs?

The Bible has already warned us about the state of the world. In Matthew 24:6, Jesus says,

> *"You will hear of wars and rumours of wars, but see to it that you are not alarmed. Such things must happen, but the end is still to come. Nation will rise against nation, and kingdom against kingdom. There will be famines and earthquakes in various places. All these are the beginning of the birth-pains."*

We are now more aware of the world around us than any previous generation and solutions are continually being sought to find a way through all the misery and imbalance in our society. All sorts of help agencies are being set up but so many people seem to fall between the gaps in these help areas. For one reason or another they do not qualify for the help they so desperately need. The family unit is a very rare commodity these days; relationships seem to be continually breaking down. My family upbringing was very strict but at least I was given a sense of values and standards of behaviour to adhere to.

It was similar in Jesus' day. There was a clear divide between rich and poor, sighted and blind, healthy and maimed. In Matthew 26:11, Jesus says,

> *"The poor you will always have with you, but you will not always have me."*

I believe we have become complacent, apathetic, and too comfortable. We go to church on Sundays and pay lip service to God then we put Him back in His box until the next Sunday. This is not how I believe God wants us to be.

In Matthew 24:12, Jesus says,

> *"Because of the increase of wickedness, the love of most will grow cold, but whoever stands firm to the end will be saved."*

I believe God wants us to be living out our faith, a faith which is like no other because it is based on God alone not on man's creation. God needs us to help those around us. He has only our hands and hearts if we are willing to let Him use them.

Just imagine the difference to our Nation if we mobilised God's army, all believers who are willing to put God first in their lives. We can make a difference. An army is made up of individuals. Each individual has a responsibility to play his or her part. Christianity is an individual matter as well as corporate. We need each other, but above all we need a close personal relationship with God to lead us through life and touch those around us for Him.

There is a saying, "Christianity is caught not taught." People need to be able to see what a difference to the way we live our lives our faith makes. It is no good just saying what we believe, we need to act upon it in our daily living. If people see us as being no different to anybody else then why should they be interested in our faith?

So, how do we cope, what can we do? Where are the answers? In John 16:33, Jesus says,

"..In this world you will have trouble. But take heart! I have overcome the world."

It is not all "doom and gloom." I believe there is a way.

I would like to share with you my particular journey, its ups and downs and how I learned to cope, and am still learning I would hasten to add. I hope that in some way it will help you with your journey and strengthen your faith in God and your daily walk with Him.

Mary Joy

Chapter Two

I was brought up in a Christian family, and was the middle child with two brothers. My father was one of nine children and his family was well known in the locality and were looked upon as "pillars" of our local evangelical church where we also attended. My father would often speak at meetings held at the church and he helped many people.

My upbringing was very strict; I would call it Victorian in style, and a place where emotions were not shown. This eventually led to problems so that when I became angry I dared not show it lest I be "told off", and so I grew up in an environment of suppressed emotions.

However, apart from feeling angry there were times when I got very excited and these emotions I couldn't always control. It seemed that when I was showing the emotion of excitement I was put down. I remember on one occasion it was my seventh birthday. I had a party and presents and as the party got underway I got rather excited. Unfortunately my father became rather cross and the next thing I knew I was being sent to my room by my father and all my friends went home. I found this very hard to handle and didn't understand what I had done wrong.

My father had a lot of suppressed anger in him and I seemed to have the ability to trigger this anger. On one occasion he sent me to my room and then proceeded to beat me with a wooden coat-hanger across the small of my back. I remember thinking I would never be able to walk again, but I did.

My father was not all bad. I had some good times when I was older going on walks and talking with him about any subject. We also had good times of laughter. One thing my family had in abundance was a sense of humour.

My parents were not well off and so they would save up very hard so that we could have a holiday. My father had a friend at his place of work who owned a caravan and he would let us spend a holiday in it down in Selsey. We used to have lots of fun playing cricket and other ball games on the beach (it never seemed to rain then!). We would also go swimming in the sea. I was determined to swim to France in my big rubber ring – I never made it.

Occasionally we would miss the last bus home to Selsey from another town close by which we had visited for the day. We would then have to walk for miles, or so it seemed, along country lanes. My father would get us to look out for glow-worms at the side of the road in order to keep us moving along. They were happy days with good memories.

As I grew older I had piano lessons. I loved playing the Dambusters March very loudly but I am not sure others appreciated it quite as much as I did. I played the piano for our youth group on Sunday afternoons when we had a service in the vicarage or church hall. I loved playing the hymns and choruses but I did find it frustrating that I couldn't put more expression into the music. I also enjoyed singing in the church choir. I played the piano for school assembly practices and was very pleased to do this as it meant I missed a history lesson.

I was a member of the school demonstration dancing team. We would do the dances of various countries and also dress up in their costumes. We would then put on a performance for our parents and friends. We had lots of laughs during the rehearsals. The teacher, who was the deputy head of the school, was very tolerant when on one occasion my partner and I had a fit of the giggles to the extent we were unable to dance. We were just doubled over with laughter. Thankfully our teacher was rather amused and waited until we were able to carry on!

Mary Joy

Chapter Three

When I was 16 and my younger brother was 14 he developed a cyst on the wall of his brain. This brought a great deal of stress into the family and it was a difficult time. I felt very fearful but, of course, I couldn't show anything, we didn't do emotions in my family. It was a very delicate operation and we were told he could either go mad, blind or be all right. Naturally we prayed he would be all right. He survived the operation and recovered but the surgeon said at the time that after another 25 years he could have problems again. Life then went back to normal.

My younger brother grew up, got married and had four children. He eventually worked as an ambulance driver and began to train as a paramedic.

Mary Joy

Chapter Four

One holiday time I went with our church youth group to the Isle of Man on a youth holiday where we met young people from other churches. This was a milestone in my life. I used to get very uncomfortable in the meetings when they talked about a faith in God. The reason for this was I didn't think I was a Christian. This was a real problem for me because in view of how our family was regarded in our local church I felt that I had to be a Christian, it was expected of me and I spent many an uncomfortable time at meetings fearful that I would be exposed for the fraud I felt. I asked God into my life loads of times but I never felt any different. So, how could I be a Christian? One of the obstacles to my believing I was a Christian was my own church. People at my church always appeared to be smiling and saying they were fine and "praising the Lord." I knew I wasn't like that as I would feel depressed and lonely at times not always "praising the Lord" so how could I be a Christian? What a failure I felt.

It was during one of the meetings I got into quite a state and knew that I had to find out once and for all where I stood. The Bishop who was in charge of the youth holiday had said he would be in his study if anyone wanted a word with him. I quietly left the meeting (having kept at the back) and decided to go and see him. As I left the meeting and went down the stairs I started to change my mind. I was just going to turn around when the Bishop came up the stairs and said, "Oh hello, are you looking for me?"

I was trapped. So I said, "Yes, I don't believe I am a

Christian."

"Right", he said, "come to my study."

He asked me straightforward questions such as "Do you believe in God, do you believe the Bible to be God's word? Do you believe Christ died for your sins?" He asked other questions too. I answered them all with, "Yes." He said I was a Christian but lacked assurance of the fact. I repeated a prayer after him affirming my belief. After this I became aware of God in my life and I knew that I was a Christian. A peace entered me that I had never known before and I really knew that God was there.

I never looked back from that holiday; that was my starting point. In the years that followed I did experience a lot of loneliness but in those times I learned to lean on God by talking to Him as I would a friend and my relationship with God started to grow.

Chapter Five

I spent a year at college to gain higher speeds in shorthand and typing plus other secretarial skills. I found it very lonely at college, I felt different from those around me and it was hard to cope with. I prayed a lot for God to help me and He did. After a year at college I then started work as a shorthand-typist in a bank. Being in a bank I was able to get a bank loan at good rates so I bought an Austin A35 car and used to bomb around in it. I had taken my driving test when I was 17 and passed first time. With this freedom I was able to attend many Bible teaching conferences at holiday time over the next few years and these were immensely rewarding. They gave me strength to keep going. I had a lot of mountain top experiences and then the valley experiences. But with each experience I became a little stronger each time.

One day I lent my car to my younger brother. He managed to crash the car. Fortunately he was all right but the car was a write-off. This taught me a valuable lesson about possessions. That car had become too important in my life, my attitude was wrong towards it. People matter more than things. I eventually bought another car but it never had the same place in my heart that the first car did. I had learned my lesson.

I used to love to hear the organ playing in church services and on special occasions in particular. For me there was no sound like it. We used to sing all sorts of anthems in the choir. I remember on one occasion we were performing "Zadoc the Priest" at a confirmation service held at our church. The organist, our choirmaster, started the introduction; he had someone conducting the choir. Unfortunately our conductor miscounted the opening bars and brought us in two bars too soon. Our organist had a real panic but stoically managed to catch up with us and the crisis was averted. We all recovered afterwards, especially the organist who continued to be our choirmaster for some years to come.

Some years later I thought I would like to learn to play the organ and I made some enquiries about it at church. I was asked if I had passed Grade 3 piano. I said "no", my teacher died before I took the exam and I never continued with lessons after that. I was told that as I hadn't obtained Grade 3 piano I wouldn't be able to learn to play the organ. I was naturally disappointed and happened one day to share this with a family friend. This friend had built a full-size organ in his two-up-two-down cottage (the pipes were housed in his cupboard under the stairs) and he played the organ at a church regularly. He said, "What a load of nonsense, if you have some aptitude there is nothing to stop you from learning. Come and see me next week and we will see whether you can learn or not."

From then on he taught me to play the organ over a period of two years. It was difficult to practise as I didn't have an organ at home but with weekly lessons I managed.

When I had started out to work I also joined another church in New Malden, Surrey. Not long after I had finished my organ lessons, when I had managed to learn just the basic skills, I was asked to play for an Evening Prayer service at the sister church in New Malden. I was very nervous and spent a lot of time practising and getting familiar with a different organ. I also prayed like mad. I managed to cope with all the chanting and other bits and pieces and felt a great sense of achievement afterwards. I never looked back after that but continued to play in church, occasionally at the main church, learning all the time, and enjoying having the chance to play on yet another organ.

I then moved to the church of St Mary's, West Kensington. On my very first Sunday there during the Notices it was given out they were looking for organists to go on a rota for playing on Sundays. This hit me quite forcefully and I knew that was what God wanted me to do. I went up to the organist after the service. At this point I hadn't played a great deal so I told him I was rather nervous about joining the rota. Again it was quite a different organ to the ones I had previously played on.

The organist was extremely good and talented and very kind; his main job of work was as an engineer at the BBC. He suggested a service for me to play at and said he would stay with me throughout so that if at any time I felt unable to continue he would just quietly take over. Well for me that was a real challenge, I was determined not to give in and quit. I managed my first service there and afterwards played regularly there, again learning more and slowly gaining in confidence.

It was at this church that I met my future husband in the fellowship group. He was working and living in digs in London at the time.

Mary Joy

Chapter Six

In 1972 I was married in the church at West Kensington. We then moved to Maidstone, Kent to live. We attended the local evangelical church there and eventually I got involved in occasionally playing the organ. Our daughter was born here, and baptised, and I gave up work and stayed at home. This I found very hard. I had been used to working up until then and having adult company for most of the day. I found that the people around us on the estate all seemed to go to work and so I felt quite isolated and unable to make any friends locally. I found it a big change. I had no family living nearby either. People at church were very friendly but we lived a car journey away so it was not easy to meet up. I also suffered from post-natal depression but as I was told Christians don't get depressed (you know the people who say "pull yourself together") I put up with it. It made me feel lonelier than ever. But I hung in there and kept the smile on my face as best I could, stiff upper lip and all that. Eventually I did go to the doctor who put me on to some tablets which helped.

We would go to the Bible studies which were held in small groups in people's homes. We became very good friends with the couple in charge of our particular group.

A few years previously I had developed an annoying and very itchy rash on the back of my hands. It also spread to my arms and legs; whenever I felt itchy I scratched. It was very unsightly. The doctor continually prescribed a strong cream for me to use. The rash would go for a while and then return. When I was attending one of the group meetings my friend said to me that God wanted to heal what was behind this rash. I didn't really understand what she was saying and wondered what she meant.

Attending this Bible study was another turning point for me. On this particular occasion they talked a lot about the Holy Spirit. In my evangelical teachings nothing much was said about the work of the Holy Spirit in a Christian's life. So I became interested. After church one Sunday when I got home I said to my husband, "If the Bible tells me about the Holy Spirit then that's OK."

I found an old book of my father's which had a chapter on the Holy Spirit with a load of scripture references. I settled down in the afternoon and as I looked up all these scripture references it was as if scales fell from my eyes. I had read the Bible for years but had never noticed how active the Holy Spirit was and who He was. The Bible showed how vital the Holy Spirit is in a Christian's life. He is the engine for a Christian, the source of power needed to live through each day. This was another milestone in my Christian life. God showed me the truth I needed to see and learn.

I know that before doing this Bible study I was very suspicious when I heard people talk of the Holy Spirit, mainly because I did not understand. I know of occasions when people had gone "over the top" about God's Holy Spirit and had been very "happy clappy" and not had their "feet on the ground" and seemed divorced from reality. They saw themselves as being superior to other Christians. I believed this to be very wrong. As I have discovered, the Holy Spirit is there for every Christian to equip them for service. It doesn't mean that we become superspiritual; it means that we are properly equipped to do God's work as

He intends us to do it, not in our human strength, which would not be effective anyway, but in the strength given to us by the Holy Spirit. We do not stop being human because God's Holy Spirit resides in us. The Holy Spirit is sent to be our guide, helper and counsellor and to help us in our daily living. His job is to direct our attention in worship to God and God alone. He will also convict us of sin in order for us to keep our relationship right with God.

I would like to share just a few scriptures which spoke very clearly to me of the Holy Spirit's importance in a Christian's life.

Before Jesus was crucified he told his disciples that he would not leave them on their own but would send them a helper. John 14:26,

> *"But the Counsellor, the Holy Spirit, whom the Father will send in my name, will teach you all things and will remind you of everything I have said to you."*

It is interesting to note that the Holy Spirit was to remind the disciples of everything Jesus had said to them. We also read in 2 Timothy 3:16-17,

> *"All Scripture is God-breathed and is useful for teaching, rebuking, correcting and training in righteousness, so that the man of God may be thoroughly equipped for every good work."*

The scriptures have been given to us as a living word from God, this makes the Bible unique – it is not man-made but God-breathed.

When Jesus was living here on earth doing His Father's work He received the Holy Spirit to equip Him for the work God sent Him to do. If Jesus needed the Holy Spirit how much more do we need him? Luke 3:22,

> *"...and the Holy Spirit descended on him in bodily form like a dove. And a voice came from heaven: 'You are my Son, whom I love; with you I am well pleased'."*

When I first attended church with my family, as I mentioned before, we had no teaching on the Holy Spirit, it seemed a taboo subject. I discovered that it is the Holy Spirit that gives life to my faith; I can't function properly without him. God equipped Jesus with the power of the Holy Spirit. When Jesus died on the cross it wasn't until after He had risen from the dead that He sent God's Holy Spirit to dwell among us. The disciples were told to wait until they "received power from on high." Jesus appeared to His disciples after He had risen to tell them to wait until they were equipped; Acts 1:8,

> *"But you will receive power when the Holy Spirit comes on you; and you will be my witnesses in Jerusalem, and in all Judea and Samaria, and to the ends of the earth."*

I have found that I cannot witness or live the Christian life by my own efforts. It is only with God's help and the equipment He provides can I achieve anything for God.

I am limited by my human abilities and strength but with God He can take me beyond my abilities and give me another dimension, which is spiritual, through the power of His Holy Spirit. He alone enables me to live the Christian life so that it makes a difference wherever I am.

Chapter Seven

God also tells me what spiritual fruit I should be bearing. In Galatians 5:22-26 we read,

> *"But the fruit of the Spirit is love, joy, peace, patience, kindness, goodness, faithfulness, gentleness and self-control. Against such things there is no law. Those who belong to Christ Jesus have crucified the sinful nature with its passions and desires. Since we live by the Spirit, let us keep in step with the Spirit. Let us not become conceited, provoking and envying each other."*

The fruit of the Spirit is referred to as one whole fruit not fruits of the Spirit. As a Christian my aim is to grow in love, joy, peace, kindness, goodness, faithfulness, gentleness and self-control. How much this fruit is needed to be seen in action in our world today to offset all the cruelty and pain people are suffering one way or another.

Another description used by Jesus of a vine is very descriptive. John 15:1-2,

> *"I am the true vine, and my Father is the gardener. He cuts off every branch in me that bears no fruit, while every branch that does bear fruit he prunes so that it will be even more fruitful."*

Here is a warning that if I don't bear fruit for God then I will be cut off, but in order to bear good fruit I will need to be pruned. Pruning is not a pleasant experience, it can be painful and feel harsh at times but God knows what areas in my life need to be removed which hinder my relationship with Him. In John's gospel it tells of where my spiritual strength comes from and the importance of maintaining my relationship with God. John 15:5-8,

> *"I am the vine; you are the branches. If a man remains in me and I in him, he will bear much fruit; apart from me you can do nothing.*
>
> *"If anyone does not remain in me, he is like a branch that is thrown away and withers; such branches are picked up, thrown into the fire and burned. If you remain in me and my words remain in you, ask whatever you wish, and it will be given you. This is to my Father's glory, that you bear much fruit, showing yourselves to be my disciples."*

I grow fruit in my garden. At first I have to make sure it is well fertilised and kept watered. After the blossom has come the fruit sets and then the fruit starts to appear, very tiny at first. As well as the right weather conditions the fruit tree needs the right aftercare. In order to serve God I need to make sure I am grounded firmly in Him, that I stay part of the vine because it is there the strength and power of God passes through to me. I receive all the nutrients I need for my spiritual health. I cannot do anything without God and need constant feeding from His word and His presence.

When the blossom appears on the tree it needs the conditions to be right long enough for the fruit to set properly. This can be a difficult stage as a lot depends on the weather as to how long the blossom stays on the tree. Some blossom will be lost resulting in lost fruit. The important thing is that the small buds of fruit remaining on the tree are looked after and nurtured until they are able to reach their full potential.

Before a branch grows thick and strong it starts off as a small twig. It is very vulnerable at this stage. So I have found it is spiritually.

When I started off in the Christian life I was very vulnerable and had a lot of learning to do and experience to gain. I can only learn as much as I allow God to be involved in my life and this can only happen if I stay attached to God. However, I am still vulnerable today but as time goes on God gives me the wisdom I need and the protection I need to live each day for Him. I am learning to use the equipment provided by God, namely the armour of God to protect myself against God's enemy and mine, the devil. Make no mistake, the devil does exist.

A vine and other fruit trees have a dormant period, a resting period before they start the whole cycle of producing fruit again. I believe God also gives me times of rest and refreshment. This is just as essential as doing work for God. I have learned not to feel guilty any more when I say "No" to someone. I do have limits as to what I can do and it is important I keep within those so that I remain useful to God. I am no use to God in a burnt-out state. God knows what is ahead of me, I don't – He is my pacemaker.

Psalm 46:10,

"Be still, and know that I am God;"

Matthew 11:28-29,

"Come to me, all you who are weary and burdened, and I will give you rest. Take my yoke upon you and learn from me, for I am gentle and humble in heart, and you will find rest for your souls."

Isaiah 30:15,

> *"This is what the Sovereign LORD, the Holy One of Israel, says: 'In repentance and rest is your salvation, in quietness and trust is your strength…'."*

Jesus knew the importance of taking "time out."

I can say that from experience I have found by committing my time to God He enables me to use it far more effectively and efficiently than I would on my own. God is an expert on time management. He also knows when I need to stop activity and rest. God knows each one of us better than we know ourselves; He knows our limitations, strengths and weaknesses. He has given us free will to use as we choose. If we choose to do things God's way we will be considerably better for it.

I find that as I learn to trust God more each day, He keeps me occupied as much as I need to be to feel fulfilled and satisfied that I have spent my day wisely and well. God knows what my needs are; He has my life mapped out for me, one which is tailor-made. Proverbs 3:5-6,

> *"Trust in the LORD with all your heart and lean not on your own understanding; in all your ways acknowledge Him, and He will make your paths straight."*

Chapter Eight

After a while, my husband's job decentralised from London to Bristol, which meant we had to move house. So we started our search and as my husband didn't want to live too near his work we started to look at Trowbridge, Wiltshire from where he could commute to Bristol. We started looking just before our daughter was born in August 1974. I remember when we were looking for a house we drove down a particular road and we liked the look of the houses. We were looking for a four-bedroom house. As we drove down this particular road I looked at a house and quietly prayed, "That one would do us nicely, Lord." The house wasn't on the market at that time. I thought no more about it.

A couple of months later we received through the post details of a house which had come on the market and yes, you guessed, it was the one I had tossed a prayer to God about. So we came and saw it; it even had a white bathroom suite, which is what my husband wanted. It seemed just right and had a lovely big garden at the back. We put in an offer and it was accepted. A few weeks later the sellers took the house off the market. We asked them to let us know if it came back on the market. Sure enough a few weeks later it came back on the market. The end result, we bought the house and in 1975 we moved to Trowbridge.

When we were travelling down to our new house we passed a removals van on the motorway. We wondered if it was ours as it was a Pickford's lorry. The lorry didn't arrive at the house until 4pm; the lorry we passed was ours.

Apparently it had broken down on the motorway shortly after we had passed it and was therefore delayed reaching us. Whilst we were waiting for the lorry to arrive our new neighbours came and introduced themselves and brought us a cup of tea. So we had an opportunity to chat for a while. We were very glad they called on us. The house was in a filthy state. We had had central heating installed before we moved in and the engineers had left an awful mess. It was an uphill struggle getting the house habitable initially, especially with a six-month-old baby to sort out as well. It took quite a time to get some semblance of order into the house but at least it was a good time of year and not the middle of winter.

Chapter Nine

We had no relations living in Trowbridge. We started looking for a church to attend in the area and found an evangelical church just round the corner.

People were very friendly at the church. One lady in particular was very kind. As my husband was away at work from early morning until evening it began to get a bit lonely again. This dear lady started popping in occasionally with little gifts. I shall never forget her kindness and friendship. To me she was a lifeline in those early days. I used to love watching the Wimbledon tennis and one day my lady friend invited me round to her house one afternoon. She then settled down to play with my daughter and suggested I might like to go and watch some tennis on the television for a while with her father-in-law. She was very thoughtful. She also did a beautiful drawing of our daughter which we still have.

Eventually we settled down and started to make friends within the church. So things were looking up. I joined various groups in the church and was glad to attend a mother and toddler group held in the vicarage. People at last with whom I could speak and share!

One Sunday my kind lady friend introduced me to another lady at the church. She made the comment that she thought that this lady and I would become good friends one day. What that lady knew or saw I shall never know but she was exactly right. I have been friends with this lady for over 30 years and continue to be.

Well things were really starting to look good. Then it happened. My daughter tended to cry a lot and being a new mum I didn't always know why. I tried all the usual things but then the crying really started to grate on me. Suddenly I felt anger rising up from within me. The force of it frightened me, and I started to shake my daughter. I then realised what I was doing and dashed upstairs with her and placed her in the cot, put the side up, went downstairs and telephoned my (new) friend. I must say this experience showed me how easy it would be to take it out on the baby. I thank God He had His hand on me and my daughter.

As a result of a chat with my friend I went to see her and her husband one evening to talk and pray about what had happened. At the time my friend and her husband were praying for people when the need arose (they have been involved in the healing prayer ministry now for over 30 years). I was added to the list.

That first evening was the start of my healing journey with God. This was not a comfortable time but I knew I needed God's healing touch in my life and the only way forward was with His help. More about that later.

After a while I became pregnant again and our first son was born in October 1976. I had difficulty trying to feed my son, especially with a toddler to look after, and I developed a breast abscess which became extremely painful. I was also busy trying to get things together for Christmas as the in-laws were coming down to stay over the period. I went to see my doctor and he told me that I had to rest as much as possible, hoping that the rest would cure the abscess. Well with in-laws coming I felt I couldn't just leave everything as I had to get food sorted out and the presents. It was very difficult to find time to rest. I regularly visited the doctor and things were not improving. Eventually, about a couple of weeks before Christmas my doctor insisted that I put my feet up and just rest. So I rushed home, baked some mince pies and then proceeded to try to rest, whilst coping with a toddler and a few-weeks-old baby! I never thought to ask for help, I was too bogged down with everything.

Christmas Day came; the in-laws were with us. I managed to cook the dinner, with help, but when I sat down at the table to eat I just keeled over in extreme pain. In the end my husband had to call the doctor. She was very good and came straight away. As soon as she examined me she said, "Right, straight to hospital you will have to have this abscess removed."

So I landed up in hospital on Christmas Day.

I was going to be operated on that evening but more emergencies came in so I was put on the back burner until the next day.

When the surgeon had done the operation and came to see me he said he had never seen such a big abscess and didn't know how I had coped with the pain. Well, I didn't know either.

Whilst I was in hospital more people were added to our ward. They had as few wards open as possible. As a result another patient and I landed up at the bottom end of the ward and then when there was no more room our beds were wheeled out into the general rest area where the television was. This room was absolutely freezing as it was like a conservatory, mostly glass. The heating made very little difference. At the time there was snow on the ground. I found the food very hard to cope with. As soon as I got a whiff of it I couldn't eat it. As a result I landed up in hospital for two weeks. I couldn't leave until I had built my strength up, having two children at home to cope with, so I had to eat. They even managed to ruin a simple rice pudding. During my stay in hospital I didn't see the children which I found very difficult. My in-laws had kindly stayed on after Christmas in order to look after them but they had to return to their home some time.

I came home from hospital in a bit of a sorry state but at least I was home and could eat good food. I was so weak that I couldn't even hold my son and bottle feed him. So how was I going to cope? I didn't know, but God did.

I had made good friends at our church and they turned up trumps. They came and fed my son until I was strong enough to do it, they cleaned the house and they brought us cooked meals. I shall never forget their kindnesses. I would not have coped without them.

I also had to visit the hospital for check ups and again my friends would come and look after the children. On one occasion I was being driven back from the hospital during the heavy snow. We got stuck at The Viaduct Pub near Winsley. My driver was very nervous and kept asking me to "stay put" as if I was going to run off somewhere – where I don't know and considering I didn't have any strength it would have been impossible. I managed to ring home to warn my friend that we were held up by the snow and she very kindly waited until either I returned or my husband did from work. She had her own family to cope with but despite this she was very generous with her time and practical support for which I was extremely grateful.

I eventually got back to some form of normality and life then settled down into a routine and we continued to build up a network of friends.

When we joined the church they had an elderly organist. She was becoming very frail. I used to go and talk to her and we had many a chat and laugh and I had shared about my playing the organ. One day she said to me, "I have had enough now, you take over playing the organ."

I had a word with the vicar about this, passing on what the organist had said. I had to be careful that this lady did not feel I was pushing her out in any way – she may have had second thoughts later on. Eventually she wrote a letter to the vicar resigning and I was asked to take over. So for three years I was the organist and really enjoyed playing. My repertoire of actual pieces of music was not very good. I had not had much time to learn. I used to play choruses before and after the service. In due course I managed to find time to start to learn some pieces much to the relief of one particular lady in the congregation. She would constantly come and see me after the service and suggest pieces of music I could play before and after. She had no idea about the pressures I had in bringing up the children whilst coping with a full-time organist post.

At least I had learned the Wedding March for weddings!

Mary Joy

Chapter Ten

My in-laws, after visiting us several times, decided that they liked Wiltshire and eventually moved to a house a couple of roads away from us. This was the first time we had ever had relations living near us. They also came to the same church as us. This wasn't always easy but we managed to co-exist at church and they were very involved in the church life and didn't have a great deal of time with the children as they were attending meetings and going for days out round and about.

I would now like to jump back in time a bit to when I was first married. My husband and I came from very different upbringings. We were both working full-time before the children came along. I remember I used to get very angry and would simmer inside when after a day's work I would come home to get the evening meal. My husband when he came home promptly sat down in a chair and read a book. After our meal he would then go back to reading his book. I used to mutter to myself, bang things around to get his attention but he was completely oblivious. I thought, "Why should I do it all, I am out at work all day too, why isn't he helping me?"

As I've said before, we never showed much emotion in my family, it was kept under wraps, so I wasn't the sort who would throw pots and pans at him, just around him!

The problem was our different upbringings. I didn't understand this until some years later. In my upbringing my father and mother worked as a team. They helped each other when necessary. I was used to seeing my father doing the decorating, keeping the family accounts, doing the gardening. My mother would do the chores in the house. My father was involved in our upbringing and used to play with us and shared looking after us. I remember on one occasion I longed to paint and so when my father was decorating the hall and landing I decided I was going to paint my bedroom door. When my father came home he was furious I had painted my door but he soon calmed down when he inspected it. There were no runs or drips; in fact he actually said I had done a good job. That was high praise indeed as he was a bit of a perfectionist with his decorating.

In my husband's upbringing it was a different story. His mother did not go out to work. She ran the household, doing as well as the chores the decorating and gardening and the accounts. My husband's father would come home from work in the evening and just sit and read or watch the television, or else he would go outside and potter or do "something" in the garage! His mother waited on him. My husband's father was not overly involved with the children either, that was mother's job.

As you can see the upbringings were quite different so when we married these two different patterns of upbringing were brought together under one roof. I now understood what was going on. My husband was just behaving as he had seen his father behave. His father was his role model so he couldn't see anything wrong with it. Why should he?

Just before our daughter was born I said to my husband that I wanted him involved with his children as I believed he should be, they were his as well as mine. When our daughter was born he did start to become involved and as she grew he would read her stories and play with her and then he would play with our other children when they were born.

Our second son was born six years after our first son in November 1982. By this time I was 37 years of age and my doctor was concerned about the pregnancy. I was very fatigued during it and felt as if I was dragging myself around. It was very difficult coping with the other two children as well. I was still playing the organ at church until it became too difficult. After his birth I still wasn't feeling too good. I didn't seem to have any energy. I was seeing the doctor regularly who was quite concerned. She knew there was something not quite right but couldn't make out what it was. I found I kept becoming quite breathless but didn't understand why. One day my closest friend mentioned to me that there was a speaker coming to a meeting in Bath, would I like to go. I said if I can manage to drive there "yes" (she didn't drive). I managed to get us to Bath without mishap but I found the car very heavy to drive.

When we arrived at the meeting I had to sit down as I felt so unwell. It was a lady speaker. I don't remember much about the actual meeting except that at the end people were invited to go forward for a healing touch from God. I went forward with my friend, not knowing what to expect and I felt quite nervous. We all stood in front of the rostrum and she prayed for us all that God would touch us. Then she said something else which I heard just as I fell to the floor. She said, "There is someone here whose heart God is healing tonight." I knew that was me. It might sound a bit drastic this falling to the floor. I didn't hurt myself and I did not feel any fear at all. As I lay on the floor I could hear what was going on around me but I couldn't move. As I lay there I felt a pricking sensation in my chest. I believe God operated on me that night whilst I was lying down and the pricking sensation was my chest being sown up afterwards by God's gentle hands.

When I was able to move I got up and literally staggered back to my chair, I felt almost drunk and couldn't stop giggling. My friend, of course, joined in giggling with me, she couldn't help it. I felt quite light-headed. By the end of the meeting I seemed to be back to normal. There was a difference though. When we left in the car as I started driving I mentioned to my friend that the car felt very light to drive. When I got home, the very next day I vacuumed the house from top to bottom and wasn't at all out of breath.

I then had a doctor's appointment, what was I going to say? As soon as I entered her room at the surgery her first comment to me was, "My, you do look well what has happened to you?"

I said, "Well, I don't know whether you will believe me but God has healed me?"

She said, "Oh I do, what happened?"

I told her what had taken place. She could see that I was so much better and was very pleased and accepted my story. She also suggested that I had my heart checked out to see that all was well which I agreed to do. This reminded me of the time when Jesus healed a man and then told him to go and show himself to the high priest. Because I was only 37 they never considered checking my heart. They probably wouldn't have found anything anyway as it was like an intermittent fault caused by a faulty heart valve. I remember my father had had some heart trouble when he was younger and this sort of thing can be hereditary.

When my second son was born I found it too much to cope with being an organist at our church as it was a big commitment so I relinquished the post so that I could look after my three children.

When the children were young we really needed a holiday. Money was pretty tight at the time but I knew I would be able to save up enough to cover the holiday but the problem was getting the deposit together in time. So I didn't say anything to anyone and prayed to God and asked Him if He could enable me to get the deposit. To my surprise and delight, a few days later an envelope was pushed through our letter box. In it was the exact amount we needed for the deposit. I never knew who it was from and I respected their wish for anonymity. God is good. He knew we needed the break and He provided for us.

Mary Joy

Chapter Eleven

When my children were born and growing up it was at a time when it was usual for mothers to stay at home and look after them.

I got to a point as they became older that I needed more than just being at home. I found it too isolating and needed the company of other adults. I also needed to do more than run a home. My in-laws were very disapproving of my going out to work because my husband's mother had been at home all the time. This was regarded as being a bad mother. I was going against the trend. It made me feel very guilty but I knew it was right for me and I subsequently found that I was able to cope a lot better with the children when I had interests outside the home. I didn't become so bogged down with everything.

My confidence level at this time was very low, having been out of the working environment since 1974 which was 16 years at home. We had a little shopping mall in the town and in that mall there was a Christian bookshop. I knew I had to start somewhere and I approached the owner, who I knew, to see whether I could do a few hours. He was very happy for me to do that and I worked on a voluntary basis. The shop layout was such that I could take my youngest son with me. He would play on the floor of the unit whilst I looked after the shop. I was extremely shaky at first and wondered if I would cope but I asked for God's help. Gradually my confidence started to return. When my youngest son started play group and then infant school I was able to do a bit more. These were my first tentative steps towards getting back into the work scene. Doing voluntary work, however, did not help my sense of worth. I still felt a lot lacking and needed to move on.

I was originally a shorthand-typist and eventually became a secretary in the days of the manual and electric typewriter. Times had moved on and there were now computers and word processors.

I knew that if I wanted to return to work I would have to update my skills and so I joined a class in the town to learn word processing and took exams. Having successfully passed the necessary exams I was ready to venture out into the workplace and be a bit more ambitious. I was still very nervous. It wasn't just the work but it was running the home as well and learning to fit everything in.

When I had progressed enough I applied to some agencies for part-time work. I remember the very first place I went to was a solicitor's office. The agency thought I would be suited to this particular job as it was of a confidential nature. I had been involved in a lot of confidential work when I was in banking. When I arrived at this office I was taken upstairs into a big office with no one else in it. I was then confronted with a strange looking typewriter I had never seen before. It had a narrow screen stretched across the front of the carriage. The screen was, I discovered, a word processor. I felt as if the word processing training I had done hadn't done me much good. However, I was given a document to type out which couldn't have any mistakes in it. I started off trying to master this strange machine. I kept making mistakes so had to start again, and again.

I prayed like mad that God would help me get this document typed. The wastepaper basket looked rather full by lunchtime and I was not much further forward. In despair I went to lunch still praying, asking God to help me. When I returned from lunch I thought well Lord I am not going to be defeated by this document I am going to get it typed. So I kept praying for help and started off again. Eventually I did get the document typed and felt such a sense of achievement I was quite chuffed with myself and I thanked God for enabling me to do it. This of course was a boost to my confidence.

After working in the solicitor's office I was sent to an insurance firm in Bradford-on-Avon. This started off as filing one day a week. How the filing could take all day I could never understand as I finished it in half a day. I then asked if there was anything else I could do as I still had the rest of the day for which I was being paid. They asked me if I could type. I said yes and so I was sat down in front of a computer. They also gave me a tape. I hadn't used a Dictaphone much before so this was also a learning curve. When I sat down in front of the computer, alas it was a different system to the one I had learned. So they taught me their system. This was again a confidence booster.

I then started to fill in for that firm during holidays and at other times when they were extra busy. My confidence continued to grow. After a while I was offered a job on their staff but I turned it down as I felt it wasn't the right place for me. The salary was also on the low side and I knew for my sense of self-worth it was important that I felt I was paid what I believed would be right for me.

By this time I was searching the papers for jobs. I went for several interviews which came to nothing. However, it was not wasted time as after each interview my confidence continued to grow. I learned in the interviews how people perceived my abilities which I found very encouraging.

One day I saw a part-time job advertised working 18½ hours in a legal department at the local Council. I felt quite overwhelmed by the advertisement because I wasn't sure whether I would be up to the job. The job description sounded so involved so I prayed about it and then in faith applied for it. I had the worst interview I have ever had. The person who interviewed me kept a deadpan face throughout the interview, no reaction from him whatsoever. I struggled to find questions to ask. At the end of the interview they said they would be notifying me of the outcome. Well, after that I thought that was the end of that – nothing doing there. God had other ideas. The next day I received a telephone call telling me I had got the job. The salary was just right as well. Then panic really did set in. I was pleased and very surprised. How was I going to cope? This was my first big real job since having had the children. I reckon I must have worn God out with my prayers and anxiety.

I went for my first afternoon, people seemed very pleasant but one lady was rather cool towards me. I hadn't been there a couple of days before the Chief Executive of the Council came in to see me. He was a Christian who I had seen at several church meetings I had attended over the years but I hadn't really had anything to do with him. He welcomed me which was very nice although I don't think it went down very well with some of my work colleagues. I discovered some while later that there was a very strong anti-Christian feeling in the work place. There were various reasons for this. I knew that the people in my office would have seen my application form on which I had mentioned my various church involvements. I believe that was why I experienced a somewhat hostile atmosphere on occasions.

After my first week in this office I nearly didn't go back there the following week. I felt each day as if I was walking into a brick wall. I found that the older lady was regarded as in charge of the office and she was reacting towards me. When she was around nobody would speak to me unless it was work-related. I found this very hard to handle and so I asked for God's help. It didn't exactly help my confidence. I then decided that I was not going to be pushed out (that's what it felt like). So I embarked on a counter-attack. Whenever I was in the room on my own with another colleague I would start chatting to them and getting to know them. Eventually I spoke to all of them in turn and this seemed to break down the barrier which had been there.

After a couple of years of part-time work a job in the department became vacant. It was a job I had watched another person doing and I had often thought I would like to have a go at it. It was dealing with the Council's deeds, finding out ownership of land on the map and dealing with public enquiries and entering land details on a computer system. I then went and spoke to my solicitor boss and asked him if I could work full-time. Eventually he came up with a plan. He asked me if I would be interested in taking on another part-time job to make mine up to full-time. I said I would be happy to do that seeing as the job he offered me was the job I had been very interested in. God was good. This gave me very good variety in my work.

Soon after I became full-time the older lady in the office decided to retire. Systems were being changed for new, more efficient ones and she wasn't happy with the changes and so she left. The atmosphere changed quite dramatically then and we used to have a lot of laughs.

Mary Joy

Chapter Twelve

L ife was looking good again. The children were growing up and moving on. A few years ago my daughter was married and then my younger son was married. Lastly our elder son got married so all three now lived away from home.

I retired from work when I was 60. A few months prior to retiring I committed my retirement into God's hands and asked him to show me how he wanted me to spend my time. I still wanted to be involved with people in some way.

For several years, whilst I was still working, I would take a short service at our local nursing home once a month. I was also playing the organ on occasions, helping out at different churches when the need arose as well as at our own church.

As I prayed I had the name Dorothy House Hospice come to my mind. As the months passed this stayed with me and I felt God wanted me to apply to them as a volunteer. When I actually retired I first applied to become a bereavement counsellor. I had a very lengthy interview and learned what was involved. I didn't feel it was quite right. There was a lot of work involved, more than I felt was right for me. They didn't consider it would be right for me either.

I went on the induction course still not sure whereabouts in the organisation God wanted me to be. I was beginning by this time to favour helping out in the Day Patient Unit but wasn't sure if they had any vacancies. After the induction course we each had an opportunity to talk to the Volunteers' Manager. She asked me what I wanted to do. I said I just wanted to be involved with people in some way. She then suggested the Day Patient Unit and said she would look into it. Just before Christmas I helped with putting a mailshot in envelopes, this was an opportunity to meet more volunteers.

The Manager then came back to me later and said there was a vacancy in the Day Patient Unit if I would like it. That is where I now work and it is very rewarding. We see people who are very ill but show great courage. We have lots of laughs and the nurses and doctors help them and work in conjunction with the person's GP and the hospital. Many make new friends and it helps them to be able to share their situations with each other. They can also spend time doing art projects and crafts which they seem to enjoy. Some discover they have abilities which they hadn't realised before. They can also do life stories. With help, they compile their own story with text and pictures. This is a means of leaving something behind for grieving relatives and friends to look at. We also take patients out and about. When the weather is good we often go for a walk in the beautiful grounds.

As well as attending Dorothy House, I felt God wanted me to do more at the local nursing home where I took a service once a month. I went to see the Manager and she was delighted. I now go there as a volunteer and visit the residents, especially those who do not get any visitors. It is very rewarding. Some like to have a chat, others just like me to pop my head round the door and say hello. It all depends on how they are feeling so I have to be sensitive towards them and not stay too long. I still take the monthly service with a band of faithful helpers.

There are also occasions when the residents have a sing

song and I go and play the piano for them. We also take a carol service at Christmas which they enjoy, especially the mulled wine and mince pies afterwards. I also help out on outings by taking charge of one of the wheelchairs. It is quite an art steering these chairs and on my first occasion, much to my occupant's delight, I nearly demolished a row of neatly arranged shoes on the bottom row of a display in Marks & Spencer! It gave us a good laugh.

I had since a young girl wanted to become a nurse. I always felt within me a desire to help people in some way. It seems that after all these years God has opened up a way for me to fulfil that desire, not as a nurse but, by giving me an opportunity to care for others.

I am still being given opportunities to play the organ and help out at local churches when the need arises for services, funerals and occasional weddings.

Mary Joy

Chapter Thirteen

As I mentioned earlier my family background comprised, in part, suppressed emotions. God saw it was time for me to be healed and set free from the chains of the past.

My first time of being prayed for was about my anger which I saw later was covering a lot of other emotions but the anger had to be dealt with first.

I visited my friends again and we waited on God. I felt the need to be able to squeeze something. I was given a pillow which I was able to squeeze to help me get in touch with my anger. As I squeezed the pillow I felt the anger again and as it came up I was able to let it out – the pillow got a real beating but boy did I start to feel better, although rather exhausted. The anger had to come out and I was able to let it out in a controlled and safe environment. The only harm done was when I opened my eyes and looked around, there were all these feathers flying around in the air. I had shredded the cover of the pillow so finely that all the innards of the pillow came out. At least we were able to laugh about it. God was very gracious. But this showed me how strong and dangerous my suppressed anger was.

Over a period of time I gradually released all the anger within me until it was all spent and cleansed away by prayer. But what was behind the anger? I didn't become angry without a reason or reasons. Over a period of years I have been prayed for what was behind the anger. I had a lot of anger towards my parents and this I had to be willing to let go of and give to God. I had to forgive my parents. It wasn't easy but with God's help I managed it. So the healing process continued. As I received my healing gradually over the years so my energy level improved. It takes an enormous amount of energy to keep our emotions suppressed. It also made me feel quite unwell at times too. I found these ministry sessions were spaced out. God knows how much we can cope with at any one time. There were times when it seemed just too much, but God knew better and of course He was always right.

God was always there with me and I felt safe in that knowledge. Another interesting fact was that the rash I had on my hands and arms started to disappear and heal up. What my friend in Maidstone said all those years ago was right. As I received God's healing for my dis-ease within, so He healed my diseased hands and arms, the rash appeared to be an outward sign of my inner dis-ease.

I was never able to share what God had done for me with my parents. They just would not have understood and it would have caused more trouble than healing.

Chapter Fourteen

I had a lot of laughs with my mother over the years; she had a good sense of humour. We used to go to the C&A shop and try on the hats, posing in front of the mirrors. We would become quite hysterical with laughter looking at the sight of us. Yes there were times of laughter too. My mother retired when she was 60 having worked for many years for the electricity board. My father was also now retired. We didn't see much of them at this time. She had always had trouble with being overweight and had tried for years to lose some but was unsuccessful. As time passed she became unwell and in a great deal of pain but she still wouldn't go to the doctor. Having had previous bad experience of doctors she wouldn't go and see one. At this time I was married with three children. My youngest was around two years old and so when my father asked me to come and see her I took him with me. My father wanted her to see the doctor but she wouldn't go so he asked me to persuade her. I had a talk with mum and eventually she agreed to see the doctor. She was immediately rushed to hospital and operated on. They discovered she had ovarian cancer and she died six months later.

When she was ill in hospital she called me to her bedside and asked me to keep an eye on dad. I said I would. She then returned home where she died three months later. My husband and I managed to get down to see her before she died to say our goodbyes. My husband and I left the children with the in-laws and arrived at my parents' home around 1pm. Mother had been unconscious most of the time. Shortly after we arrived she suddenly opened her eyes, took a long look at me and then closed her eyes again. She never regained consciousness after that. It was as if she was waiting to see me. At 5:30 that evening she died peacefully and I remember looking out of the window and seeing a beautiful sunset, which seemed rather fitting.

Unfortunately after my mother's death my father didn't want anything to do with me or my family. This made it very difficult as my mother had asked me to keep an eye on him. I used to telephone him on a regular basis to see that he was all right but he started to be very unpleasant on the telephone. I found this very hurtful. Every time I rang him I was coping with rejection from him. In the end I had to stop telephoning him because it became too damaging to me. I had to forgive him and managed to do so eventually, with God's help. This situation prevailed to the day of his death. The children found this very hard and hurtful. My father cut himself off from everyone except he did allow my elder brother and his wife to see him very occasionally. He even turned away his own brother who tried to reach him. He was also quite rude to his neighbours and this was sad because they kindly kept an eye on him. One day they noticed he hadn't taken in his milk. They rang the police and together they went into the bungalow. Dad was lying on the floor in the living room. The doctor said he wouldn't have suffered, he just collapsed and died. I was very thankful for this as I didn't like the thought of him having a lingering death with no one around to care for him.

Chapter Fifteen

As predicted by the surgeon my younger brother became ill again, and yes it was actually 25 years later, as the surgeon had said. He developed a cyst on his pituitary gland. He was back in hospital and underwent three major operations in six months. The nurses and doctors were amazed at how he survived this. He then had two attacks of meningitis. During the last attack he was rushed to hospital but they were unable to raise his blood pressure. I was very thankful that they couldn't revive him because he had suffered so much and his quality of life was not at all good.

He eventually died at age 43. I went to see him a couple of months before he died. I knew I was saying my goodbyes. As our conversation came to a close, in my mind I had a picture of him stepping on to a wooden bridge, turning to look at me and then walking over the bridge. I shall never forget the memory; it was one of peace and I knew that he had arrived safely in God's hands where there would be no more sickness or disease for him but a new heavenly body.

I was glad that my brother did not die before my mother because I don't think she would have coped at all well. My father did not attend the funeral. He remained cut off from the family which people found very hard to understand.

Chapter Sixteen

After a lot of prayer and careful consideration we felt God was leading us to attend another church in Trowbridge having been at our present one for about 18 years. That's when I encountered more difficulties.

I had been brought up all my life in an evangelical church environment, although I wasn't particularly comfortable in it, it was all I knew at the time. Going to this new church, I found to be a very big step into the unknown. Leaving a church environment which I had always known gave me a real sense of insecurity but now God was moving me out of my comfort zone into a new area for my life. What next I thought!

When we started going to the church the people were very friendly and welcoming to us. Our close friends had also moved to the church at the same time. The church was a little high (much higher than the evangelical!) but I didn't really mind that. They had candles, wow! Although the evangelical church did not go on candles I really liked them and felt they were an excellent symbol of God's light. Perhaps a bit of high churchmanship was lurking in me somewhere.

As we settled down in the church I started to feel very lonely and cut off again. I couldn't understand why. People were very friendly so what was wrong? After much prayer and seeking God I saw a picture of myself encased in a steel case which completely covered me. God showed me that the case represented the evangelical influence on my life. It was like living in a straitjacket. I had become a person God had not intended me to be. God showed me that all the wrong attitudes and influences I had been brought up with were making up this straitjacket. It was a very painful process. Over a period of time I had to be willing to surrender to God all my wrong attitudes. This took time but gradually as God highlighted my wrong attitudes I surrendered them to Him and began to feel a lot freer, and not so lonely. I was beginning to relate to people better because God took away my judgmental thoughts and my pride. I started becoming the person God had intended me to be.

The church choir consisted of boys and men but later on it changed to both men and women so I was able to join. Eventually, after many years of not playing, I had the opportunity to play the organ again. I now help out occasionally at several churches. I believe God has given me a gift in organ playing which He wants me to keep using. God's hand has been on me over the years. He has given me the opportunity to develop my musical gift in organ playing over the years. I always pray that God's spirit will move through my playing and touch others for Him.

Chapter Seventeen

For some areas of my healing I went away for weekend retreats and through the people who ministered to me I was given words from God which were of great comfort and encouragement to me. I knew God's hand was on me and that He had a purpose for my life. Throughout the entire ministry by God my walk with Him was gaining in confidence and strength. He was and is my dependable friend, guide and counsellor and I knew that whatever else happened I would never be alone because He would always be there. He would be with me in the dark places where no one else could go with me.

One of the many words given to me by God through the ministry team (in 1993) was Isaiah 61:3:7,

> "…and provide for those who grieve in Zion – to bestow on them a crown of beauty instead of ashes, the oil of gladness instead of mourning and a garment of praise instead of a spirit of despair. They will be called oaks of righteousness, a planting of the Lord for the display of His splendour.
>
> Instead of their shame my people will receive a double portion, and instead of disgrace they will rejoice in their inheritance; and so they will inherit a double portion in their land, and everlasting joy will be theirs."

I would like to quote a couple more words which were given to me during a ministry session in 1996.

Psalm 34:4-6,

"I sought the Lord and He answered me; He delivered me from all my fears. Those who look to Him are radiant; their faces are never covered with shame. This poor man called and the Lord heard him; He saved him out of all his troubles."

Psalm 25:1-3,

"To you O Lord I lift up my soul; in you I trust, O my God. Do not let me be put to shame, nor let my enemies triumph over me. No one whose hope is in you will ever be put to shame..."

These words given to me were of great comfort but I didn't quite understand the words about "shame" until a few years later.

I have found in God's goodness towards me that He only brings me face to face with past hurts when I am strong enough in Him to deal with them. This next hurt is a case in point. After all these years and many hours of receiving God's grace and healing in ministry I found my thoughts wandering back to when I was a small child and I started to feel uneasy. I felt God was asking me to look at something, and so a memory I had suppressed for over 50 years was brought back to me. I knew something bad had happened when I was very young and so sought out my close friends, who I trusted, to pray with me.

I did not find it easy but with God's help I was able to face the memory of being sexually abused by my father when I was five years old. At the time I remember trying to tell my mother, who seemed very afraid, and she wouldn't believe me. As I grew up I had wondered why I felt different from everybody else. I felt apart from others and awkward, I didn't know who I really was. I felt very insecure. I had difficulty relating to people. I invited God into the situation and received His healing. But that wasn't the end of it. I had to be able to forgive my father. It took me quite a long time. Over a period of time I had to continually keep coming back to God, saying I forgave my father and asking God to help me to mean it, from the heart. When I managed this I came into freedom.

After this ministry I started calling God my heavenly Father and have done so ever since. I am a daughter of the heavenly King. God is my Father as well as my friend.

It was after this particular ministry I then understood a lot of the words which God had given me previously. They made sense, but He knew that.

Chapter Eighteen

This brings me on to another topic. The thread that has run through my life has been the thread of forgiving. I have had to learn to forgive. When Jesus was dying on the cross he said,

"Father, forgive them…"

Jesus also said in Mark 11:25,

"And when you stand praying, if you hold anything against anyone, forgive him, so that your Father in heaven may forgive you your sins."

Forgiveness is one of the hardest things to do. When we are hurt by someone we want to hit out at them and cause them hurt. But does this make us feel any better? I believe when we do this we stay joined to that person in hurt and we feed our own hurt by hurting them. We perpetuate the hurt and we become bogged down by it. As a result we come into bondage to that person. We hear on the news about people who say they can never forgive. The person they are damaging the most by not forgiving is themselves not the perpetrator of the hurt to them.

How are we hurting ourselves by not forgiving? The hurt we hold on to eats into us making us ill and bitter, and we become a person to be avoided by others.

Jesus knew what he was talking about when He said, *"Father, forgive them."* God knows that in order for us to lead healthy, balanced lives and become the person He wants us to be we need to forgive those who wrong us, for our own health's sake, but not only for that reason. Jesus also said, "*If you hold anything against anyone, forgive them, so that your Father in heaven may forgive you your sins.*"

God's forgiveness to us is conditional on us forgiving others who have wronged us. What right do we have not to forgive others who sin against us if God is willing to forgive us our sins? We see the price of our sin in that God let go of His only Son, Jesus Christ, and turned His back on Him when He was on the cross. Why? Because Jesus was carrying my sin and yours and God being a holy God cannot look on sin and accept it. How God must have suffered to have to turn his back on His only Son, what agony He must have felt at the separation. The sufferings we go through can only teach us in a small way what suffering God felt and what Jesus suffered for us in order that we may be ransomed, healed, restored, forgiven. This is why God understands our pain. He understands my pain and brings His healing touch to restore.

As a Christian we have no right not to forgive those who "trespass against us" as this is the very foundation of our Christian faith. It is only through forgiveness we are restored to God through Jesus Christ. I am not aware of any other religion today that can forgive a person their sins and let them feel forgiven and free from the chains of the past.

Chapter Nineteen

I have spent years working hard at forgiving and it was only a short while ago that I actually understood how to go about it more effectively and quickly.

The first emotion I have had to deal with is my pride. It is pride which stops me from forgiving. I don't want to be seen to be got the better of by the perpetrator. I must win and I would do that by hitting back. Because I was proud I was unwilling to bend to the will of God. Jesus said, "Forgive"; I said, "Not yet Lord, I just want to take a few more swipes at him/her first."

I have to be willing to let go of my pride by handing it over to God to be cleansed away.

Secondly, it's a question of "willingness." Once I have laid aside my pride I come to the matter of my will. I do not believe that in my natural state I am able to fully forgive. I believe I need God's help. I have found that forgiving others is more a question of my saying to God, "God, I am willing to forgive this person for hurting me so badly, please give me the ability to forgive them." I am showing God my willingness to let go and release the other person from my unforgiveness. I have found that God then gives me the ability to forgive that person from my heart. God deals with my heart once I have given Him permission to do so. I still have free choice here. I start off forgiving with my mind by telling God I am willing to forgive. This is then followed by heart forgiveness which God gives me. It is submitting my will to God so that He can do the work within me.

It has taken me a long time to learn this about forgiveness but I see that God has made it clear that if we do not forgive others, we will not be forgiven.

My journey of forgiving continues because I am not perfect and we do not live in a perfect world. There are going to be times in the future when I will need to forgive. I have found that as I have forgiven people who have hurt me so my faith has become stronger, I am learning more about God and I am walking in a greater inner freedom than I have known before.

Chapter Twenty

L amentations 3:22-23,
*"Because of the Lord's great love we are not consumed,
for His compassions never fail.
They are new every morning; great is your faithfulness."*

These scriptures were given to me by the ministry team who prayed for me in 1996. That was ten years ago.

My favourite hymn is "Great is Thy Faithfulness" which is based on these scriptures. God has proved throughout my life thus far his complete dependability. God has been faithful to me; He has shown me great compassion in the healing He has brought me.

As I continue on my Christian journey I have found that God's mercies are new every morning. He gives me satisfaction, a sense of purpose and strength to cope with each day. I never know what a day may bring but I know that God has a purpose for me in each day with whomever I happen to meet or whatever I do.

Another thing I have found is that as I write this book remembering the past, I can write about it with a spirit of thankfulness. God has done so much for me for which I give Him praise and thanks. He has made my life worthwhile. He is my heavenly Father and that gives me a security within that nothing else can. I find I can remember the past without pain or any other negative feeling. This is the beauty of God's healing grace. It is only when we remember our past with pain and anger that it does us the harm. God enables me to remember in a way that is not damaging to me. People say we should forget the past. I don't agree. We can learn a lot from our past and also as we look back we can see how far we have travelled in our walk with God and how much God has forgiven and healed us. This can encourage us to "keep going." God wants us to reach our potential to become the person He intended us to be. It is a painful process because we live in a fallen world and none of us are perfect, and there will continue to be difficulties, pain and suffering. I believe there is a way to walk with God so that we can become stronger and more effective in attracting others to God. I believe the key is our individual relationship with God. Jesus never said the Christian way would be easy. In Matthew 16:24,

> *"Then Jesus said to his disciples 'If anyone would come after me, he must deny himself and take up his cross and follow me."*

An army is made up of individuals. Each individual has a responsibility before God and will be accountable to Him on the day of judgement.

It is our choice what we do with what we have been given and what happens to us as we travel through life. God has given us free choice. Every choice we make determines the road we take. We can either opt to go God's way, which is not easy and I will not say that it is but the rewards are beyond measure, or we can opt to go our own way with all that entails for us. I can guarantee that if you opt for going your own way you will never know the joy and satisfaction of a fulfilled life and of a deep relationship with the living God. Yes, we have a choice and we alone are responsible for the choice we make.

Make no mistake, Jesus will return one day. When the gospel has been preached in the whole world then the end will come (Matthew 24:14) and when he comes we are told in Matthew 24:30-31,

> *"At that time the sign of the Son of Man will appear in the sky, and all the nations of the earth will mourn. They will see the Son of Man coming on the clouds of the sky, with power and great glory.*
>
> *"And he will send his angels with a loud trumpet call, and they will gather his elect from the four winds, from one end of the heavens to the other."*

Mary Joy

Chapter Twenty-One

I believe that today we are no longer seen to be a Christian country. Despite this Christianity is still a force to be reckoned with. There are many religions in this country now but there is one very distinct aspect of Christianity that sets it apart from any other religion. The Christian religion is not "man-made."

Man-made religions are restricted to the extent of man's thinking and imagination and it is about what man does and can do within himself/herself. It is all self-effort. The Christian faith is different in that it is a gift from God. I found I couldn't earn my salvation in any way, it is a gift. Jesus did all the work for me by dying on the cross to bring me reconciliation to God. It was my choice as to whether I had God in my life or not.

Deep inside each one of us I believe there is a desire to worship something or someone. We see this around us today in the hero worship of pop stars, film stars, sports stars. We are desperate to believe in something or in someone. I have found that by having God in my life, He adds a new dimension to my way of living and my whole outlook, and satisfies that inner desire to worship and have someone to look up to.

When we were known clearly as a Christian country we had standards and values to follow. As our country has changed it has meant that no one religion must dominate but that there should be tolerance of all beliefs. This is all very well but I believe this has led to a lot of confusion, especially for young people. They are pulled this way and that by the different life styles and sets of values suggested and so they end up confused and dissatisfied. Families are falling apart, there are very few role models in family life for the young people to follow to show them how to behave and be responsible for themselves. Many are one parent families which puts untold pressures upon the one parent, trying to keep a job and run a home and look after the children. As a result children are often left to their own devices, unsupervised. One parent cannot cope properly bringing up children on their own however hard they try and may want to. Family values are fast disappearing, children seem to have no boundaries within which to grow up and develop safely. They show signs of insecurity by their behaviour and some join gangs to give them a feeling of belonging. There is a lack of respect for each other and people seem to be no longer valued. Life seems to be regarded very cheaply.

I believe that there is no better time than now for Christians to stand up for their faith. I am finding that by putting God first in my life it changes my outlook. With God in charge it helps me to see the world through His eyes. God shows me how much people are desperate to be loved and accepted for who they are, and I see how God's love can bring healing and wholeness to people. People's hearts are breaking and grieving – we see this on the news daily. People are fearful for their own safety and that of their family members. Normality doesn't seem to exist any more. The world is a cruel place. I believe as a Christian it is my responsibility to bring God into whatever situations I find myself in so that He can make a difference.

I have found that being a Christian is not a soft option, it makes me face reality. It is tough but the rewards are out of this world. I have found that when troubles come, in all sorts of guises, they can be used to strengthen my faith and teach me what I need to learn. God does not let anything happen to me that cannot be used to help me develop my relationship with Him. I have found the key is my reaction to the problems and difficulties I have to face. It is as I walk with God each day that I learn how to handle people and situations. Romans 8:28,

> *"And we know that <u>in all things</u> God works for the good of those who love him, who have been called according to his purpose" (my underlining).*

Mary Joy

Chapter Twenty-Two

O ne of the things I had to learn was the fact that even when I became a Christian I still had my human side with the ability to commit sin by thought, word and deed. The difference when I became a Christian was that I was more aware of what was right and what was wrong and the choices I had to make. This took me a while to understand.

I remember years ago when I was at work my every word and action was under scrutiny by my colleagues. They knew I went to church and was a Christian. When I slipped up in something I said they would come down on me very quickly saying, "That is not the sort of thing a Christian should say." I used to feel very guilty when this happened – I was very hard on myself. At that point I had not learned that I was still human and prone to error. The devil is the one who makes me feel guilty; this is one of his weapons against the Christian. God convicts me of my sin but the devil makes me feel guilty. I have learned since to accept the fact that I will make mistakes because I do not suddenly become perfect when I become a Christian. The world expects extremely high standards from a Christian and this was the pressure I was feeling at the time. I now realise that it takes a lifetime to grow in maturity with God.

God knows me better than anybody else, warts and all, and there is great comfort in this and a feeling of security because He loves me unconditionally, He does not stand over me in judgement and condemnation.

I have also found that being a Christian satisfies that part of me that needs to worship someone. My worship is now directed towards God where it should be. Being a Christian gives me a goal in life and that is to serve God and do things for His glory and not my own. I am still a flawed human being but as my relationship with God develops and I allow Him to have more of me, so my sinful nature is being brought under control by God and cleansed, although the process of becoming fully clean will not be finished until I reach heaven. Where the things which happened to me in my past are affecting the way I live and think, God has led me along the path of healing for my inner self by His love and grace. My healings have come about through my partnership with God, my willingness to face things I would rather not, which enabled me to receive God's healing in my emotional area, to be released to become the person He has made me to be.

There are all sorts of people who claim to heal; there are all sorts of methods used to bring people healing. I have found God to be the true healer for me. There is no aftermath with God. I have found that once God has healed me I have stayed healed, so long as I continue to live as God wants me to live and obey Him. I find it very satisfying and fulfilling living as God wants me to live and to obey Him. It isn't drudgery to obey God or burdensome. I find God makes life exciting – I never know what will happen next or what He wants me to do next. Having said that, God never gives me something to do which is outside my scope. I know many a time I have felt inadequate for the task He has given me, but God knows me intimately, better than I know myself, and knows what I am capable of. Where I lack anything in my work for God He supplies what I need. The next adventure is a case in point.

I am finding that God is using me in the musical area of our church. I was approached by a friend at church and asked if I would be interested in helping to set up and run a singing/instrumental group for a Taizé service as part of our church outreach. I knew God wanted me involved so I said "yes." Then panic set in. Although I am musical and I have done a lot of playing the piano and organ over the years I have never done anything like this. I have only had an occasional opportunity to lead a choir practice at church which again was a first for me and quite nerve-racking but I believe the choir practices I took were a part of God training me for what was ahead, although I didn't know it at the time.

My friend and I started to plan and prepare for the service. We committed everything to God and prayed before we did anything. The preparations seemed to take on a momentum of their own. We prayed for the people we needed and gradually we built up the singers and instrumentalists from our church and other churches. The practices were my main challenge as it was an area in which I was not overly confident. The reason for this was because when I learned to play the piano years ago I never took my Grade 3 exam. Consequently I missed out on a lot of music theory. I have picked up a lot over the years but I found it a bit unnerving taking these practices with people in the group who had far more musical knowledge than me. However, I persevered. I asked God every time to help me when I took the practices and He always enabled me to take them successfully, despite my lack of knowledge. He provided me and equipped me with what I needed. For me this was a step of faith and I suspect this won't be the last service I shall be involved in. God wants to use my gifts in music and I know He will equip me with whatever I may need and encourage me to move forward in this area.

I have shared this to show you that when we commit our lives to God He knows exactly what we are able to do and what our desires are. God alone can help us to fulfil the desires we have which are for the good of others as well as ourselves. In committing my retirement to God He knows exactly what I need to be doing with my time, the most effective use of it and the satisfaction gained.

This is one of the exciting aspects of being a Christian. There is always something for us to do and as we travel along God opens up the way for us into areas where we can grow and develop. There is always some new challenge around the corner for us.

Chapter Twenty-Three

I have seen that we are all on a journey together and that is the beauty of being a part of a Christian church. We are there for each other. There are in the church some Christians further along the road than others. It means there is a wealth of experience to draw on so that we can help each other along the road.

We hear a lot today about people's rights but very little about people's responsibilities. I believe as a Christian I have a very definite responsibility to other people. I have the responsibility to spread the good news of the Christian faith. People are so bombarded with words these days I believe it is by living my faith each day that it should speak for itself to others. People should be drawn to God by seeing Him in me and other Christians as we go about our daily lives.

God has a job tailor-made for me which only I can do, and that is where my responsibility is.

I am continuing to learn the importance and power of prayer. We see in the gospels how Jesus was very committed to praying to His Father in heaven. He would frequently withdraw to a quiet place and spend time with His Father in prayer. Jesus knew the importance of prayer and the strengthening He gained from these times. I am in constant conversation with my heavenly Father throughout the day, I bring Him into everything I do, chatting to him as a friend.

It was through the power of prayer that I received God's healing.

I am a member of our prayer ministry team at church and we always pray in pairs. We have people asking for all sorts of things. We come alongside the person in need and meet them where they are. We then pray for whatever they ask for. It is then up to God what happens next. Sometimes God will illuminate something to the person. Some people come in just to talk over something which is bothering them. With all the noise and rushing around in today's society people are crying out to be listened to, to be heard. This, I believe, is a very important part of the ministry. We need to be available to help people along the way. At the time it may not seem much that we pray for but God uses whatever He wills to bring people to himself. God can see the whole picture of the person we are praying for not just the part we can see. In Isaiah 55:8-9,

> *"For my thoughts are not your thoughts, neither are your ways my ways," declares the LORD.*
>
> *"As the heavens are higher than the earth, so are my ways higher than your ways and my thoughts than your thoughts."*

I have also found that by praying regularly to God I am continually strengthened and can live and move under His protection. We are living in dangerous times and God's protection is very important. The devil is alive and well, he is the prince of this world but his time of ruling the earth is limited by God. The devil has been defeated by God through the cross and Jesus rising again from the dead. I have also found the need to read and study God's word; this is my spiritual food to build me up and equip me. I also need the armour of God to wear for protection each day. This is my heavenly armour of protection against the enemy the devil. I am fighting a spiritual battle so need spiritual equipment to protect me in the fight, as set out in Ephesians 6:10-16,

> *"Finally, be strong in the Lord and in his mighty power. Put on the full armour of God so that you can take your stand against the devil's schemes. For our struggle is not against flesh and blood, but against the rulers, against the authorities, against the powers of this dark world and against the spiritual forces of evil in the heavenly realms.*
>
> *"Therefore put on the full armour of God, so that when the day of evil comes, you may be able to stand your ground, and after you have done everything, to stand.*
>
> *"Stand firm then, with the belt of truth buckled round your waist, with the breastplate of righteousness in place, and with your feet fitted with the readiness that comes from the gospel of peace.*
>
> *In addition to all this, take up the shield of faith, with which you can extinguish all the flaming arrows of the evil one."*

I have the power of almighty God at my disposal. God gives me all the equipment I need for the battle, it is mine for the asking. If a soldier goes to war ill-equipped then he doesn't stand much chance of survival. God knows what I need in order to win the battle. God has won the ultimate battle but I have skirmishes to cope with here on earth. I know I am on the victory side. Yes, the devil can make life very difficult for me and unpleasant at times but God only allows what He can use to teach me and strengthen me in my faith. One of the devil's biggest cons in the world today is to convince people that he doesn't exist. As a Christian I know that he is alive and well but remember that he is defeated and that the power of the cross and resurrection of

Jesus is where he was defeated and that is where my victory over the devil lies.

Chapter Twenty-Four

Over the years I have been learning to trust God more and in over 40 years I have found God to be faithful in every way. Through life's ups and downs I have found God to be there for me, helping me, lifting me up, healing me and helping me to move forward. His mercies are new every morning. I can have my sins forgiven each day so that I start the next day with a fresh clean sheet. He gives me strength to keep going and my hope is in Him. The peace God gives is sure and steadfast and with God I don't know what a day may bring but I can face it with Him. He is my guide through life's maze and my eternal hope.

Great is Thy faithfulness, O God my Father,
there is no shadow of turning with Thee;
Though changest not, Thy compassions they fail not,
As Thou hast been Thou forever wilt be.

Great is Thy faithfulness, great is Thy faithfulness

Morning by morning new mercies I see;
All I have needed Thy hand hath provided
Great is Thy faithfulness, Lord unto me.
Summer and winter and spring-time and harvest,
Sun, moon and stars in their courses above,
Join with all nature in manifold witness
To Thy great faithfulness, mercy and love.

Pardon for sin, and a peace that endureth,
Thine own dear presence to cheer and to guide;
Strength for today and bright hope for tomorrow,
Blessings all mine, with ten thousand beside.

Words: Thomas O Chisholm (1866-1960)

As a Christian I have a gospel to proclaim and the best way to do this is by the way I live my daily life. With God in charge of me it makes a difference and people notice that difference and want to know what it is. Is the cost too great? I don't think so. Life is hard for everyone but through the hardships I have God in my life with me every step of the way and that makes a huge difference.